TURNING WOODEN JEWELRY

Judy Ditmer

Photography by Douglas Congdon-Martin

77 Lower Valley Road, Atglen, PA 19310

Dedication

This book is dedicated to my mother, whose love,
faith, and generous spirit have never wavered.

Acknowledgements

I would like to thank Bonnie Klein, for generously sharing her ideas; Evelyn Snyder and Betty Scarpino, for their continuing feedback, suggestions, support, and friendship; and, of course, my mother, for reasons far too numerous to recount.

Earrings. Bradford Pear. Macassar Ebony; black onyx, niobium, porcelain, brass, blackstone. 2.5" x 1.125".

Printed in China
ISBN: 0-88740-611-4
We are interested in hearing from authors with book ideas on related topics.

Published by Schiffer Publishing Ltd.
77 Lower Valley Road
Atglen, PA 19310
Please write for a free catalog.
This book may be purchased from the publisher.
Please include $2.95 postage.
Try your bookstore first.

Contents

Introduction

I started making earrings because like most of us who earn a living at our craft I quickly discovered the necessity of having small, inexpensive items to sell at shows and to wholesale to shops and galleries. Jewelry made sense from several perspectives. People would buy it as gifts for friends as well as for their own use, it met the criteria of being small and inexpensive, and it would be easy to pack and ship for wholesale orders. And people already know they buy earrings; they need only decide whether to buy MY earrings.

From this humble beginning in exigency has come continuing growth and discovery. Making these small sculptures - for that is what they truly are, since virtually the only constraint on their design is that they must fit on an ear and hang properly - has furnished endless opportunity to explore form and space, color and line, iteration and contrast. I have come to appreciate the process of making this jewelry for the design potential as well as for the sales. This is more than simply making a virtue out of necessity. The work has not only led to answers for some of the original questions (I now make and sell several hundred pairs of earrings each year), but to new questions. These questions, in turn, have led to further growth and new work. The possibilities I have found in this form are far more varied than I had imagined they would be. Thus my expectations have expanded, and, consequently, my work has also improved and deepened, for seldom will attainment exceed expectation.

It may well be that you are simply looking for a good idea for a few gifts, or for something a little different to try out some weekend in the shop. In this book you will find what you need to do that. I hope you will also find an encouragement for further exploration. This book is presented not merely as a plan for a specific project, but as a tour guide as well. From the ideas presented here, design your own itinerary. Approach the making of these pieces as a kind of adventure--as play--and you may find more than just another project. Remember to be playful and to have fun!

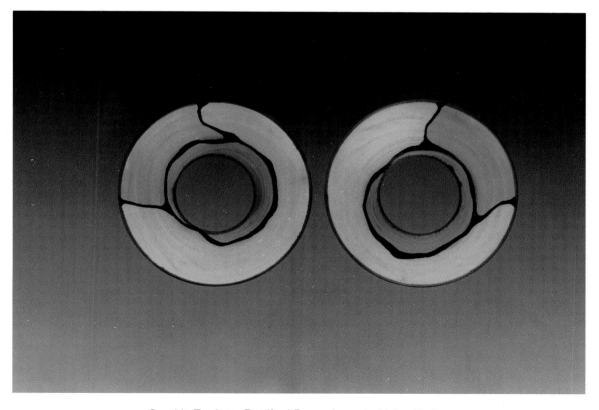

Graphic Earrings. Bradford Pear; pigmented inks. 2" dia.

Before You Begin

Materials

I like to say the turnings these earrings are made from are not really tiny bowls, but rather very, very short, very, very fat spindles. That is to say, the "dishes" are turned into the end grain of the wood rather than the flat grain, as is usual for a bowl. Therefore, dense, hard close-grained woods will work best. After some practice, you will find it easier to get a clean cut in difficult woods, but in the beginning it would be best to use only sound, dense, hard wood. Most exotics such as ebony, rosewoods, tulip wood, moradillo and the like are good - although brittle or splintery ones such as purpleheart or wenge are troublesome. Among domestics, dogwood and fruitwoods of all sorts (excepting perhaps cherry) are usually excellent. Many odd little shrubby trees and ornamentals provide very good material - I have used (and would be glad to again, if I could find) swamp privet, American hornbeam, lilac, blackhaw, rose-of-sharon, persimmon, apricot, redbud and many other lesser known woods. Keep an eye out for these as they often turn beautifully and have unique color and grain.

Supplies

Findings (earwires, posts, headpins, etc.) and other supplies for making jewelry are available from a multitude of sources. It is beyond the scope of this book to list such sources, but here are a few suggestions for locating suppliers.

If you are in or near a large city, you will probably be able to find a bead shop nearby which will have many findings available, as well as an amazing variety of beads. Also there may be good craft supply stores. Most smaller towns will have a fabric store, and many of these carry some findings. Mail order is a rich source of supply. Go to a good bookstore, purchase current copies of several craft and jewelry publications, and peruse the ads and classifieds. Usually the ad will contain information about the types of items carried, charges for catalog and price list, etc., which will help you decide which suppliers you might want to use.

Equipment and Tools

You will need a lathe, and although the pieces you will be making are small, a large, heavy lathe is best. There is considerable stress applied to the work in turning the pieces for these earrings, especially laterally in parting the pieces off. A heavy duty spindle and bearings will reduce vibration problems greatly. If you must use a smaller, lighter lathe, you should start with shorter pieces, take smaller cuts, and exercise great care in parting off.

You will need a bandsaw or various hand saws for preparing rough stock and for cutting the discs.

Necessary turning tools include a medium-to-large spindle gouge and parting tool for roughing out the cylinders from which the pieces are to be turned, and a small spindle gouge and parting tool (which are specially ground--more about this in the text) for turning and parting off the discs.

Various other small tools and supplies are discussed in the appropriate parts of the text.

A Safety Reminder

Woodturning can be dangerous. Be certain that you know how to use equipment and tools in a safe manner, and keep safety in mind at all times. Don't use any tool in a manner inconsistent with its intended purpose. Always wear eye and face protection, and use some form of dust collection or filtering mask. Specific safety tips or concerns in the text are identified with a:

Please pay attention to them.

Making the Jewelry

Cut the stock to length. I suggest a piece 3" to 6" long. A longer piece results in less waste and fewer mountings, but is initially more difficult to turn due to vibration. So start with short pieces; work your way up to longer ones as your skills improve.

Use the bandsaw to cut an "X" in the end of the piece for centering. It's not necessary to cut corner-to-corner. It's safer and easier to cut with the flat of the stock on the table.

Since I'm going to turn this into a cylinder for jewelry, the exact dimension is not critical, so I just "eyeball" it. For some projects, such as a spindle with a square base, it would be important to be very accurate.

While I'm at the bandsaw I prepare several pieces of turning stock.

Again, cut the stock to length.

SAFETY TIP: When cutting round or irregular stock to length, it is very important to provide support under the leading edge of the rough piece, or the blade may grab and yank the piece forward - sometimes violently. At best this will bend or break the blade; at worst it may pull your hand into the blade. Use a wedge of waste wood or a V-shaped cradle of wood to support any piece which does not have a flat surface to sit securely on the saw table.

The tailstock holds a "live" center. This turns on a bearing as the wood spins. A fixed or "dead" center tends to burn the wood as it turns and may not support it as well.

Mount the wood between the centers, using the X's as guides to center the wood.

The spurs of the drive center go into the lines of the "X" we cut at the bandsaw. This roughly centers the piece.

Turn the wood down to a cylinder.

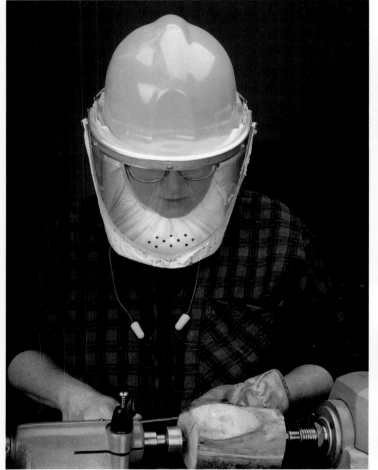

You can rest the tool gently on the spinning piece to see if it is round. If the tool bounces, the piece is not yet round.

SAFETY TIP: Proper safety, including breathing protection, is critical. I am wearing a filtering apparatus with a helmet and face-shield assembly. This device pumps filtered air from a battery-pack/filter assembly worn on the waist, up through a hose into the helmet, across the face and out the bottom. The face mask is very important, because turning can create dangerous projectiles. Don't turn without a face shield! Safety glasses alone cannot protect your face from flying pieces, and in some cases do not even adequately protect your eyes.

SAFETY TIP: Be sure the tip of the tool is well out in front so it can't catch.

6

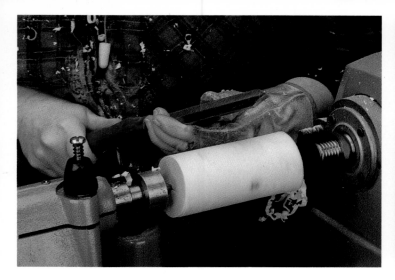

When the cylinder is completely rounded, switch to a parting tool.

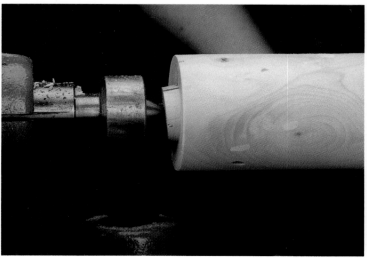

The spigot should taper slightly, getting larger toward the body of the piece.

Use this to create a spigot at one end.

Move on to another blank.

SAFETY TIP: After mounting the piece between the centers it is a good idea to spin it by hand before turning on the lathe, to make sure there is clearance all around. If the piece hits the tool rest when you turn on the lathe, it can do serious damage certainly to the wood and maybe to you.

A couple of passes should create a spigot about 3/16" to 1/4" long. The diameter is not critical, as the piece will be individually fitted to the waste block; around 1" to 1 1/4" is good.

Repeat the process.

At this stage you want a smooth, even surface with no tear-out. Sanding will come later.

This angle gives you a better view of the use of the spindle gouge. The flute points in the direction the gouge is moving; cutting takes place below the center point of the cutting edge.

Another view of the parting tool. Make the parting cut by resting the bevel of the tool on the cylinder and gently raising the handle of the tool. This lowers the cutting edge into the wood. Continue to the finished diameter.

Attach a waste block to a faceplate. The waste block should be dry hardwood - poplar or maple will work and are not expensive - about 3 1/2" in diameter (or the diameter of the faceplate) and 1 1/2" to 2" thick. Put screws in all the holes - you need as much support as possible to reduce potential vibration problems.

Shape the waste block to a flattened dome by rounding the corner off...

continuing the curve...

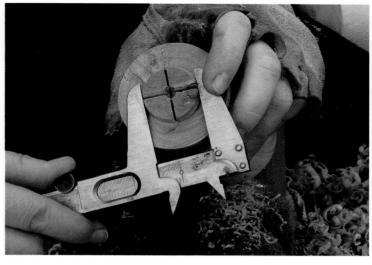

down to the faceplate. It doesn't have to be a particular shape, just get rid of all the corners and flats so you won't whack your knuckles if you brush against it later while it's spinning.

With a metal caliper, transfer the diameter of the spigot...

Flatten the end.

to the flat of the waste block.

SAFETY TIP: You should have the point of the caliper which is left of center (i.e., on the downward-rotating side of the piece) resting on the tool rest and lightly touching the wood to mark it. The other point must **not** touch the wood. Use it only to sight the mark you've made with the first point. If the wood grabs the right point, it will yank it up and throw it over and down against the tool rest - maybe injuring your hand and most likely damaging the caliper.

The result.

On the flat of the waste block, begin to create a socket for the spigot by working from the center...

out to the mark you have established with the caliper. (I found the thickness of the waste block was contributing vibration so I shortened it before finishing the socket.)

This will check the fit. If it is close, you can just push firmly on the piece for a few seconds, creating a burnt but tight fit.

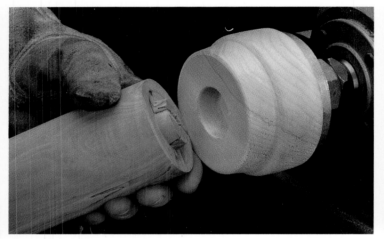

The socket should be deeper than the spigot is long, and tapered toward the bottom.

SAFETY TIP: If the spigot bottoms out in the hole, it can yank the piece of wood out of your hands as you are checking the fit.

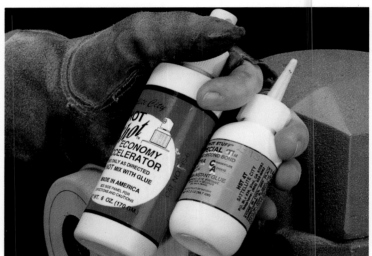

I use a cyanoacrylate glue with an accelerator to hold the blank to the waste block. Use the ultra gap-filling glue to help fill any minor irregularities in the fit.

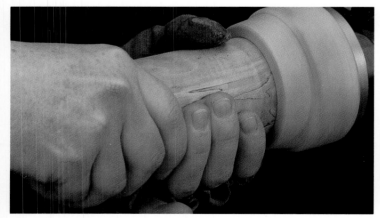

Hold the piece firmly in both hands and push it into the socket while the waste block is turning.

Spray the waste block with accelerator. This makes the glue set up much more quickly.

Apply glue to the blank.

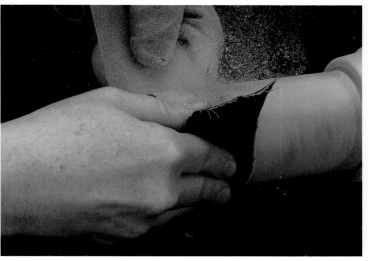

Sand the cylinder with 120, then 180 grit paper.

Turn the piece quickly by hand to spread the glue...

This should give a nice smooth surface. Since this will be the edge of the earring and very thin, it is not necessary to go into very fine grits.

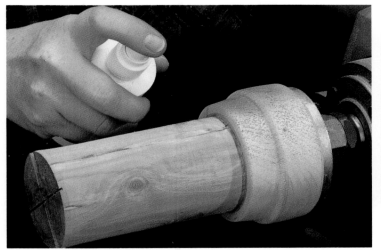

and spray the glue that squeezes out around the edge with accelerator. You want just enough glue coming out to know that you have good coverage at the joint. The glue sets quickly, but it's best to wait a minute or so to be sure it is completely set before turning on the lathe; otherwise uncured glue may be flung out at your face.

To cut the "dish" I use a small spindle gouge which I have ground back on the sides to a "fingernail" shape. The extended edge makes it possible to use more and different angles while cutting with the tool. Here you can see my gouge (top) compared to a gouge fresh from the factory. You should also gently round the back of the tool where the bevel meets the body of the tool. This prevents the sharp end of the freshly-ground bevel from marring the surface as it trails the cut.

Cut from the outside edge in. First you are just getting rid of the bandsaw marks and any tear-out left on the end.

Just inside the edge start the finishing cut with the tool edge straight up and down. This prevents kick-back.

Turn a concave surface on the end of the cylinder. I generally do a roughing cut...

Work toward the center, gradually turning the flute of the gouge up...

followed by a finishing cut. The roughing cut takes more wood and is done faster; the finishing cut takes a small amount of wood and is done more slowly. Begin the final cut by using the part of the edge that is left of center to make a very gentle scraping cut into the edge of the cylinder face, no more than 1/16" wide. This will give a surface for the bevel to ride as you begin the finish cut. With practice, you may not need to do this step - you will acquire enough control of the tool to be able to start the cut at the very edge.

as you go. You should move the handle of the tool gently and steadily towards your left as you go in. This will help establish a smooth, even curve.

As you move to the center, the upper side of the tip of the tool is doing the cutting. This cut takes some practice, but as you begin to get the hang of it, you will be able to get a very clean cut.

Separating the turned disc is done with a specially ground parting tool. It has a tiny point at the right side of the cutting edge (as seen from the top). This is made by letting the right side hang very slightly over the edge of the grinding wheel as you touch up the bottom bevel.

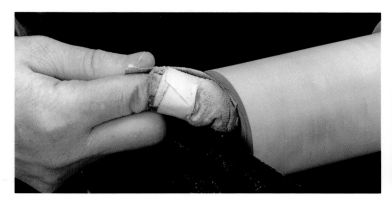

Sand with 280-grit paper...coarser if necessary, although I have found that if you need coarser paper than about 220-grit then there is usually too much tearing of the wood fibers for any amount of sanding to eliminate. Keep practicing to cut cleanly.

The top bevel is longer than the bottom bevel, which means that the cutting edge is below the center line of the tool.

SAFETY TIP: This prevents the tool from being jerked sideways by the force of the wood rotating against the edge, which could cause a dangerous grab.

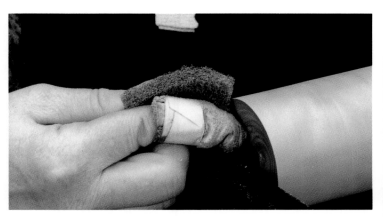

Follow the sandpaper with Micro-Fine Bear-Tex™ finishing pads. This material is superior to steel wool because it will not break down in use as steel wool does, it does not rust, and it won't leave bits of fiber in the wood as steel wool can do. Be sure to complete sanding and polishing while the lathe is on. If you try to do anything to the turned surface after the piece is off the lathe, it will mar the polished finish.

Begin by turning the tool upside-down and using the point to score the wood about as far back from the edge as the depth of the dish. This cuts the fibers of the wood and prevents tear-out which would mar the edge of the next disc. You need to cut only about 1/16" deep to do this.

With the parting tool turned right side up (the point on the right and the long bevel on top), work back toward the scored line. You are essentially cutting clearance space for the tool to make the final, finishing cut. The quality of the cut is not crucial until you are close to what will be the final surface.

Make a smooth finishing cut. Hold the tool firmly and follow the curve of the inside of the disc by gently and steadily swinging the tool handle around as you cut in toward the center.

Deepen the cuts, being sure to follow the curve of the disc.

A final cut separates the disc from the cylinder. You may need to make an additional clearance cut before this final parting off.

Work your way deeper, but leave enough material in the center to support the piece as you make the finish cut on the outer part of the disc.

Continue with a variety of woods until you have several types of discs from which to create your jewelry.

Another way of treating the surface of the discs is chatterwork. I begin by turning several smooth sections on the end of the cylinder.

Hold the tool firmly against the rest and touch the cutting edge with medium pressure against the wood. I do this at around 1000 rpm, but you will want to experiment to see what speed works best for you.

The result. There is a slight cone in the center.

Polish with the Bear-Tex™ pad. This will smooth the surface without losing any detail.

The chatter tool has a heavy body and a thin blade. The body rides on the tool rest, and the blade hangs over and vibrates, or "chatters". This tool allows you to extend the blade to varying degrees from the body, which gives different effects to the chatterwork. It's fun to experiment. For chattering, you will need very dense, close-grained wood, such as ebony. Softer woods will not leave a cleanly chattered surface.

I often add accent lines with the gouge after doing the chatterwork. This gives definition to the segments.

It's like putting a frame around a picture.

The result.

Use the same technique as before to part off the disc. With the chatterwork, the disc is usually not quite as deeply curved, so the back will be flatter as well.

Some of the discs - those which will be used with the convex side showing or which need to have a hole turned in the center -will need to be turned on the "back", or convex side. To do this, you need to build a simple jig. I'm using what remains of the waste block and turning a convex surface. I leave the spigot hole; in fact, I smooth the edge of it with a small bevel. This will prevent the tool grabbing and yanking the workpiece off (or breaking it) when you cut through while making a hole in the disc.

The curve of the jig should be slightly flatter than the curve of the discs so they will meet at the outside edge but not in the center. The clearance hole in the jig also helps here.

I cut a series of guide lines to help the eye in centering each workpiece. These consist of three heavy lines...

with three lighter lines between. Spacing is not important. You'll just use whichever line has a diameter slightly larger than the disc you're mounting.

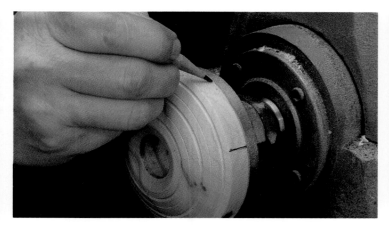

Make twelve marks around the outside edge of the jig. They do not need to be precisely spaced, approximately even is good enough.

Drill a hole at each point for a screw.

Drive in the screws so they are secure, but with enough protruding (about 1/2" is good) to wrap a piece of elastic around them.

Double a piece of 1/8" elastic and...

tie the loose ends around one of the screws.

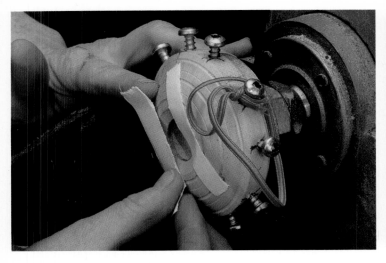

Lay two strips of double-faced tape across the jig. Make them thin enough that they don't entirely cover the surface. You need to be able to see the guide lines. Also, if the disc is taped solidly all around, it may be difficult to pull it off when you're finished turning it.

The piece mounted for cutting a center hole.

SAFETY TIP: Be very careful not to get your hand anywhere near the outside of the jig while it is spinning. The protruding screws can do a lot of damage to your hand if you should happen to brush against them.

Lay the disc on the jig, using the guide lines to center it. Gently press the edge down all around. If you press in the middle it may crack the disc.

Reinforce the hold by stretching the elastic across the edge, looping the elastic around whichever screws will hold it in the right place. The combination of the tape and the elastic will hold the disc in place, as long as you don't get too aggressive in cutting!

Use the gouge to open the center. Be careful to start the cut inside the elastic. Cut (gently!) from the outside in, deepening the cut slightly toward the center until...

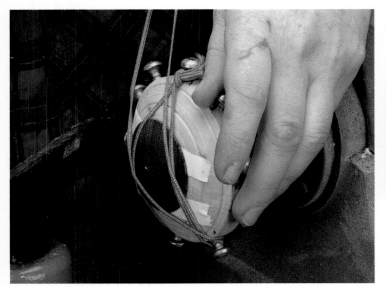

the gouge breaks through.

Use the same tool to enlarge the hole and clean up the edge. Cut with the left edge of the tool, drawing it gently outward until you reach the desired diameter. This is a scraping cut; the bevel is not rubbing.

The result.

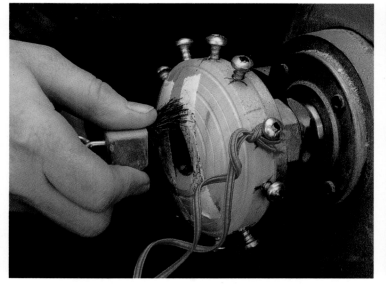

After removing the disc, use a piece of stiff brush to clean off the shavings. This will make the tape last through more re-mounts.

To get identical holes on two discs for a matched pair, mount a second disc on the jig.

Measure the hole of the first disc with the caliper...

and mark the second disc. Use a light touch or you may break the disc or tear it loose.

Cut the hole and check the size (you may want to do the measuring with the lathe turned off -it's easy to catch the caliper and spoil the piece).

Cut a "ledge" 1/16" or so wide by cutting with the left side of the tool in a gentle scraping cut. This establishes a surface for the bevel to ride as you begin the finish cut. Without this step it is difficult to start the cut without pulling the disc off the jig.

The result.

Cut across the piece with the gouge, bevel rubbing, gently following the curve. You may need to make two passes, since the cut must be very light. The slower you cut, the better the finish you will get.

The same jig can be used for cleaning up the back of the disc for earrings where this convex surface will show in the final design. The tape will hold the piece in place without the elastic so you can cut the entire surface. It is not as secure, so you must cut very lightly.

Sand with the 280-grit paper...

again followed by the Bear-Tex™ pad.

Remove any excess knobs from the center of the disc backs. This will allow the piece to move smoothly through the bandsaw when you cut them.

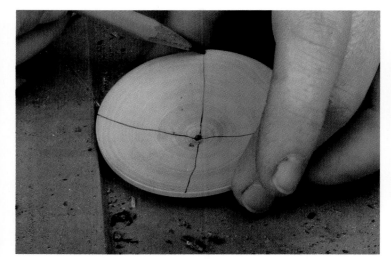

When the turning is complete you can begin to sort the pieces. Some discs will remain whole and should be put aside for now. Others will be cut into halves, quarters...

or other sections. I always mark them with a pencil where I will cut them. This allows me to make the right decision about where to cut each piece, and saves time at the bandsaw.

When you come across a flaw like this whitish spot (caused by minute tearing or bruising of fibers in the squirrely grain) you can get rid of it simply by cutting around it. Flaws in the edge are eliminated by beginning a cut there.

Some earrings (I call them double reverse) will be made by cutting two discs and turning two of the pieces over so the finished earring will have convex and concave surfaces. For these, I use a matching pair of discs which have been turned smooth on the backs. I mark an "S" curve on these discs (so the cut will encompass the flaw). The curves are mirror images.

Cut the discs with a bandsaw, following the lines you drew earlier.

 **SAFETY TIP:** Use a thin, fine-toothed blade with many teeth. Coarse blades will be far too aggressive and may break the disc or even injure you. Also, you must roll the disc as you cut. Starting with the front edge down all the way against the table, lift it as you cut so the portion of the disc at the blade is firmly against the table at all times. If you have a jigsaw, you may find it more comfortable to use than the bandsaw to cut the pieces. If you have neither machine, you could use a hand-held coping saw with a fine blade.

A wide variety of shapes and woods will allow you more possibilities for creativity in assembling the earrings.

I use four sizes of sanding drums to shape the pieces: 1 1/2", 1", 3/4" and 1/2" diameters, all 2" long. These are usually sold in sets of all four sizes. I start with the biggest, doing all the shaping that requires that size; then move to the next smaller size, and so on. Mount the drum in a chuck on the lathe. If you don't have a way to mount the drums on your lathe, you can use a drill press or a hand drill clamped to a bench.

Use the curve of the sanding drum to shape large inside curves.

This will give you uniform shapes on matched pairs.

Use the largest drum to shape outside curves by twisting the piece back and forth across the drum.

The matched pieces do not have to be 100% identical, but they should be close. Compare the shapes face-to-face.

A completed matched pair. Notice that the sanding drum is beginning to clog.

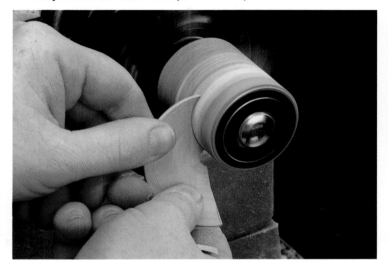

The drums can be used to create some interesting shapes.

I use carbide sleeves for my sanding drums. They are expensive compared to the paper sleeves, but worth it for my high-volume use. To clean the drum I hold a brass wire brush against it as it turns.

I give "straight" lines a gentle curve to make them more pleasing to the eye.

If there is still some clogging I stop the lathe and use a file card pulled against the direction of rotation. I also clean the sleeves occasionally with saw blade cleaner.

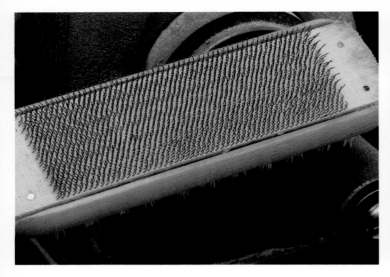

The file card.

I simply broke its mate to match...

If you are using a regular paper drum, you can use a rubber abrasive-cleaning stick.

and sanded both to a new shape.

Sometimes a piece will break during sanding like this one did. Do not despair!

The result of my serendipitous mistake.

Switch to a smaller drum for tighter curves.

The 3/4" drum, naturally, gives tighter curves.

Follow the same techniques as with the larger drum.

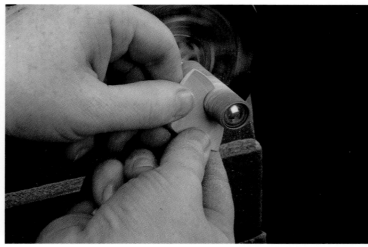

Switch to the 1/2" drum to add the final design elements. Sometimes I use this smallest drum to break up the original curve...

SAFETY TIP: Use firm, steady pressure, but don't push too hard. If the piece breaks or slips from your grasp and you are applying too much force, you may sand off some skin before you are able to pull away.

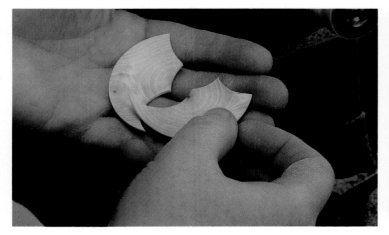

A combination of sizes of curves can create complex and interesting shapes.

or to add detail. When doing this with matched pairs, be sure to compare them often for depth and position of the shapes.

The result.

The sanding wheel smooths the shaped edges of the earring pieces. This makes them more pleasing aesthetically. Practically, it lessens the likelihood of the finish cracking at a sharp edge. Also if the piece will be colored or painted on the edge, it will be easier to do this cleanly on a sanded edge.

I use this miniature lathe to do the finish sanding of the shaped edges because I can put the machine on a table or bench and get comfortably seated for the long sanding session (I seldom do fewer than several hundred of these pieces at a time!).

The sanding wheel is made by gluing a piece of 1/4" to 3/8" thick foam to a quick release sanding disc, then gluing a disc of 120 grit sandpaper to the foam. The assembly is then mounted on the disc holder, which is mounted in a chuck on the lathe. This arrangement gives a sufficiently flexible edge to allow you to smooth the curved edges. You can prepare several discs at one time and switch them quickly as they wear out while you are working.

To sand the tight curves, begin on the flat of the edge, about 2/3 of the way into the curve, and sand to the end. If you try to do it in one stroke, the other end of the piece will get in the way.

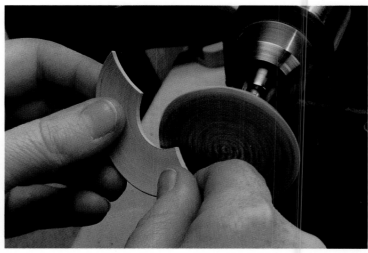

Beginning at the same point in the arc, knock off the bottom corner of the edge...

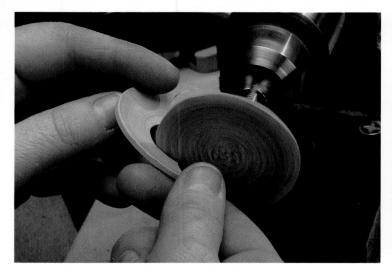

then the top corner.

and the other.

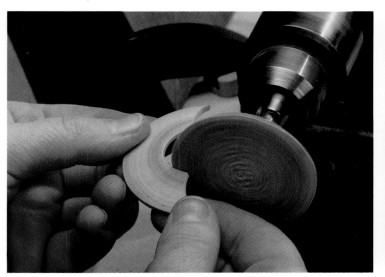

Turn the piece over and repeat the process to finish the other end of the arc. First the flat of the edge...

On flatter, more open curves it is possible to do the sanding in one stroke: first the flat...

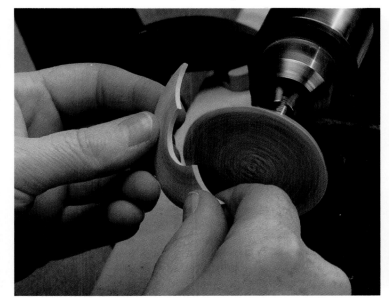

then one corner...

then one corner...

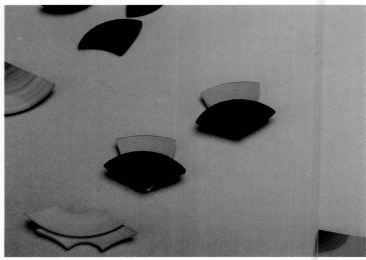

and the other.

The variations are virtually unlimited.

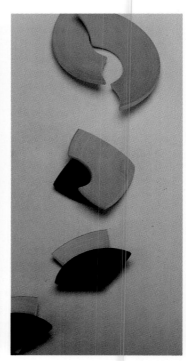

When all the pieces you have made are sanded, you have the raw material for jewelry design.

Play around. It's like a great puzzle, and you decide what the solutions are.

Sometimes contrast in texture and color is pleasing...

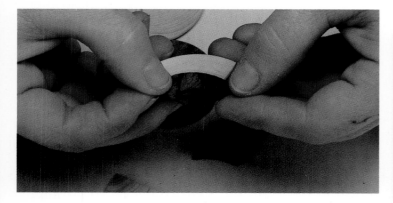

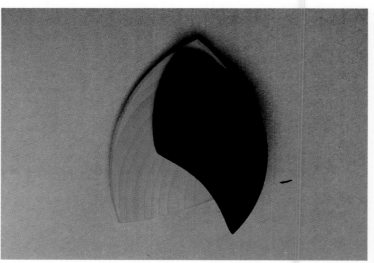

Design is simply a matter of trying various pieces together to discover interesting and beautiful combinations.

or contrasting color and related shapes or curves.

These three triangular pieces of varying size, proportion and color, placed in sequence, create the same effect.

Experiment...develop your own style.

The pieces are joined to create a variety of unique designs. This is kind of the ultimate toy for former children such as myself...the combinations possible are almost limitless.

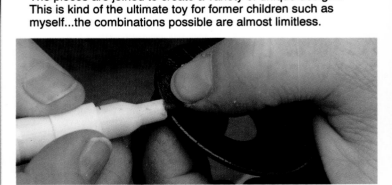

This sequence of curves in alternating directions gives the piece movement. The eye is drawn around and around the design.

Color can be added to the pieces. On dark woods I use opaque paint pens. On lighter woods any marker of the desired color will work.

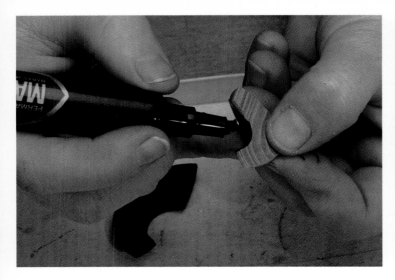

I often use black edges. They help frame the wood, help to unify different woods, and are neutral in a style sense - going with many articles of clothing.

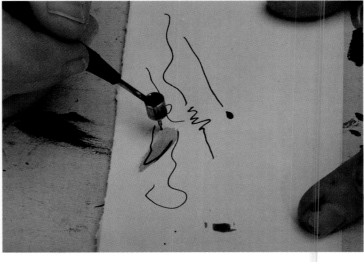

On some of the earrings (I call them graphics) I will decorate surfaces as well as edges. before doing this type, you may want to practice on a piece of paper or a scrap of wood, so you can see how the ink, paint or pigment is going to look. You can play around with color and line. The black line over the green appeals to me, so...

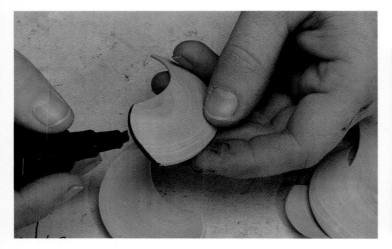

On the double reverse pieces it is important to decide how they will go together before coloring the edge. You should hold the good side up as you apply the color so you can take care against blobs on the surface that will show.

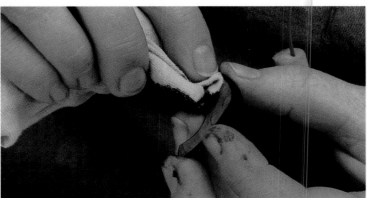

I'm going to stain a piece with green ink. I'll set it aside to dry before applying the black lines.

The edge color applied.

I'll follow the grain lines with black arcs to divide the space.

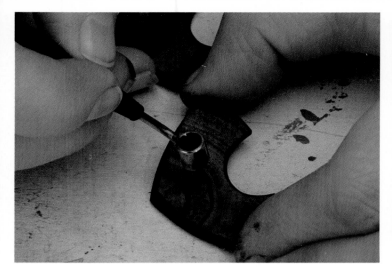

Next I'll add some dots in the spaces. Again, be playful. You'll "spoil" a few pieces, but you'll learn a lot and move toward developing your own style.

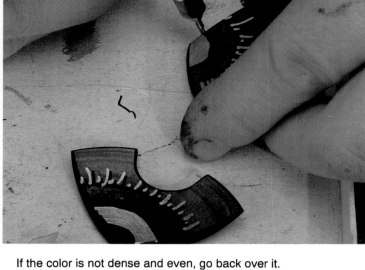

If the color is not dense and even, go back over it.

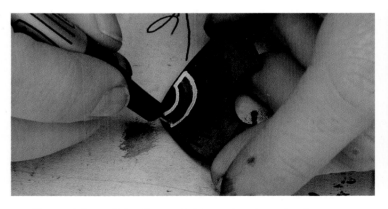

Next I add a fringe. These are creative moments. There is no prescribed way of doing this kind of thing. Use your eye and good taste. If it works, add it to your "vocabulary". You may need to touch up the lines after the ink has dried.

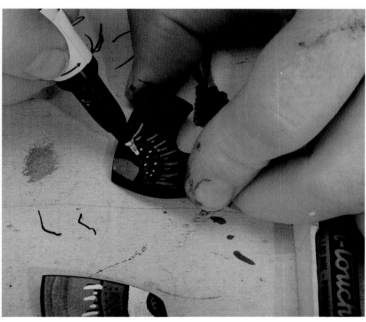

I add some white dots.

I'll try adding a little silver to brighten the piece. It seems to me that drawing the outlines first helps keep the fill from bleeding past the space you are trying to color.

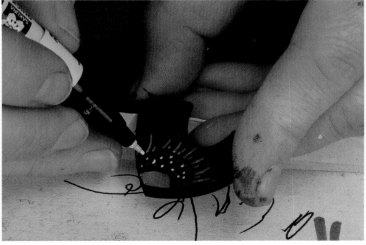

After drying, I gave the dots a second coat, because they bled into the green a little, and so were not crisp.

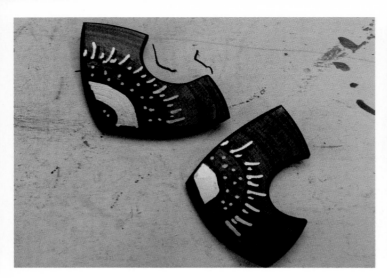

These look almost finished.

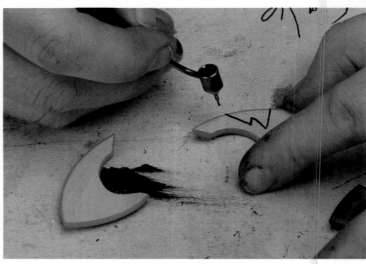

I look a piece over before drawing a design. Sometimes I will follow grain lines in dividing the space; sometimes not. But the first step is to define the spaces.

I retouch the edges.

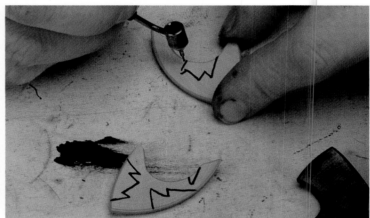

The two sides do not have to be the same, in fact it is often more interesting if they are not.

Well, maybe they're not quite finished... some purple dots spice it up a little.

The two sides.

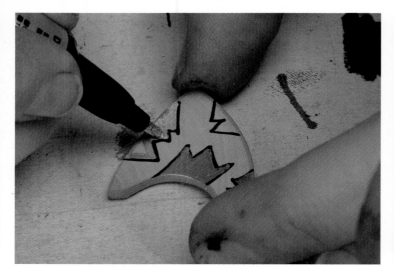

I'm going to fill the designs with silver metallic ink. I don't worry too much about going onto the black lines a little, because...

On the next pair I again follow the grain lines. As is often the case, this leads to a different design on each piece.

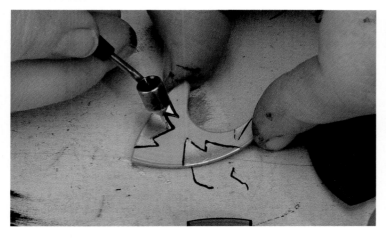

I always go back after filling the spaces and redraw the lines to make them nice and crisp.

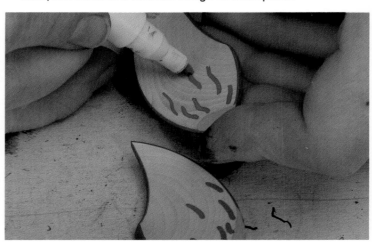

Adding some squiggles. (Ah, technical jargon!)

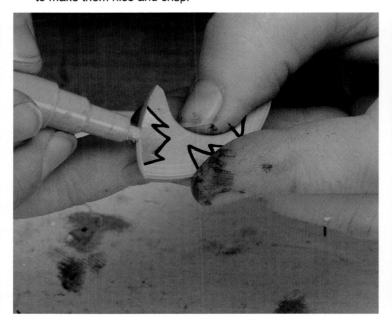

Usually after coloring and lining the pieces, the edge will need touching up.

More squiggles of another color...

and finally a few hot pink ones.

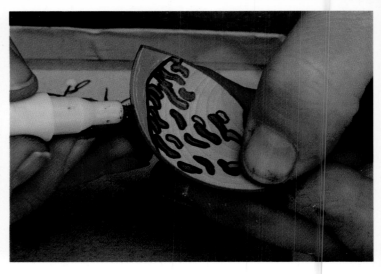

Clean up the edge by re-inking.

I let it dry for awhile before inking.

This pair has a very distinct grain pattern; I will outline it to highlight it.

Outlining the squiggles in black makes them really stand out.

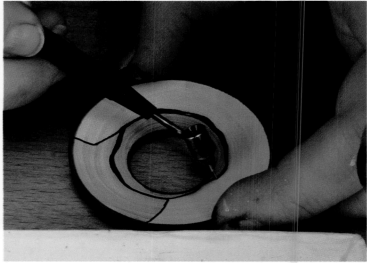

I like the simple black lines marking the color variations in the wood. They do need evening up which I do by going over them again. Sometimes the lines look more interesting if the width varies, just as growth rings and other markings in the wood will vary.

Many of the designs involve joining two or more pieces together. Hot glue from a glue gun tacks the pieces in place (I will reinforce the joints later with cyanoacrylate glue on the back). the hot glue will also bridge gaps. Apply a heavy bead...

The nice thing about the hot glue is that if you make a mistake...

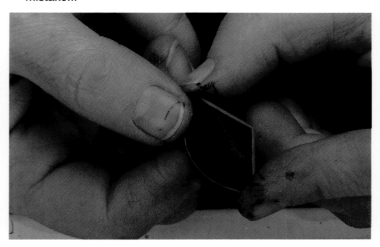

position the second piece, and hold in place. It will set up enough to hold the pieces in position in a few seconds.

you can carefully take the pieces apart, rub off the glue...

After the hot glue cools completely, you can remove any excess by gently peeling it off with a dental tool or other tool that will fit. Be careful not to scratch the surface.

and do it over.

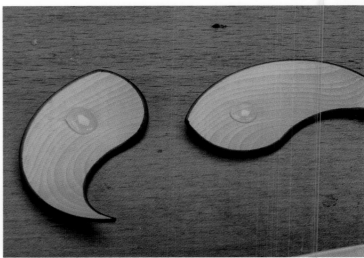

On some pieces, especially those where you will not be able to reinforce the joint from the back, you will need to use the cyanoacrylate glue. I apply accelerator to the back of the applique...

When joining two concave surfaces together it is often necessary to fill the gap by building up the glue. Place a button of glue on one side and let it set up.

and a small dab of glue to the body.

Align the other piece and place another button of glue on the back of this piece at the point where it will meet the first.

Then I lay the applique in place. Since this joint cannot be reinforced from the back, it requires the strength of the cyanoacrylate glue.

Join the two sides of the piece.

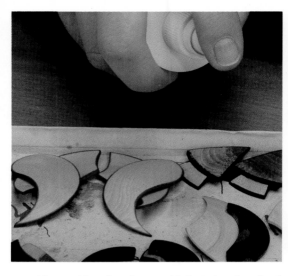

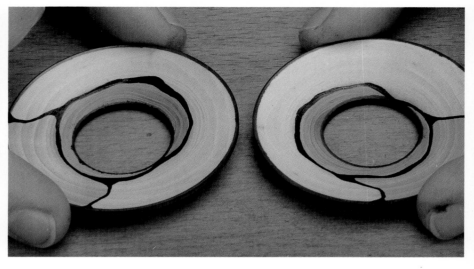

After tacking the pieces with hot glue, I make the joint more permanent with the cyanoacrylate glue. I begin by spraying the backs of the pieces with accelerator. This makes the glue set up more quickly and thus helps to prevent it from running onto the front of the piece before it sets up.

Decide how each earring should hang.

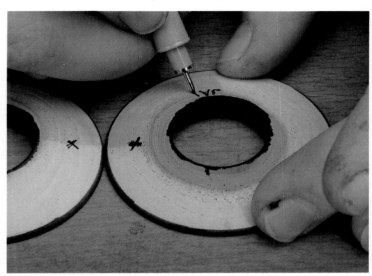

On the back of the piece I run a bead of the glue along the joint of the parts. This will reinforce the hot glue joint, and will not be visible from the front of the earring or pin. Be careful when applying the glue, as capillary action can pull the glue through to the front.

Turn the pieces over and mark the position of the posts. At this point I sign or initial the piece.

Used carefully, the glue can be built up to bridge a gap like this and create a strong union.

On pieces that are to have beads or dangles, decide where the beads will go, and mark this spot on the front.

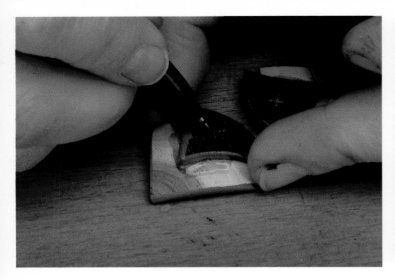

Turn over and mark for the posts.

Pins will, of course, have a pin back, but I put a post on them so they will go onto the jig I use for spray finishing. I will remove it and glue on the pin back after spraying.

Put a small drop of glue on the mark of the post. I use hot glue for this, but be advised there are many kinds of glue sticks made for glue guns; some will hold and some won't. You will need to experiment and see what works best for you. You can also use the cyanoacrylate glue, but be sure to clean the posts with the accelerator before gluing, as there is often oily residue on them (leftover from the manufacturing process) which will compromise the joint.

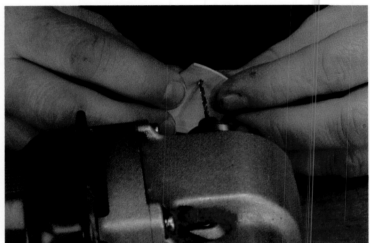

Use a 1/16" bit to drill holes for the bead dangles. I clamp the drill to a bench and hold the earring piece to drill it. Be gentle and use a sharp bit.

Hold the post in a pair of pliers and push it firmly in place. Hold it there for a few seconds while the glue sets up.

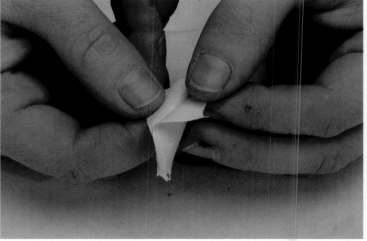

If you are spraying the pieces on a flat surface you need to lift them from the table so the finish will not be drawn under the edges where they touch the surface. This would mar the other side. You can take a small piece of double face tape...

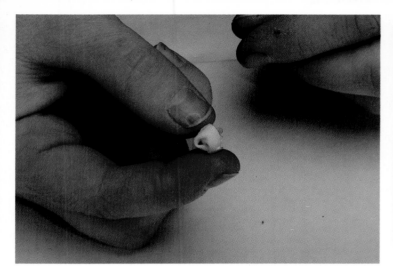

and wad it into a ball.

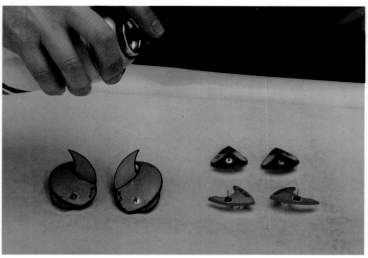

then in the perpendicular direction to ensure complete coverage. Let dry completely before doing the fronts.

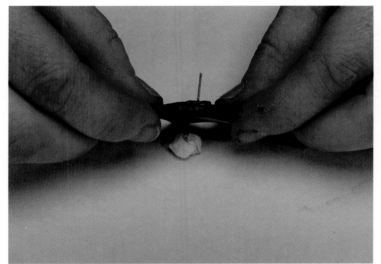

This goes on the table and the workpiece is gently pushed onto it.

Turn the pieces over, again supporting them away from the table.

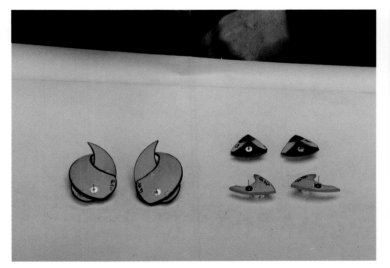

Spray the backs first, I use a semi-gloss lacquer. Because the earring is against the skin and is likely to go out in the rain from time to time, it is important to use a finish with water and oil resistance. I spray first in one direction...

Spray the fronts just as you did the backs. On the graphic pieces do a light first coat and let it dry completely before adding a second coat. This will help prevent bleeding of the colors, which can easily happen if you spray too heavily at first.

You may need to use several coats.

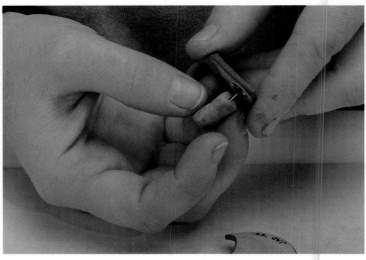

For the front, you can simply stick the post in the wad of blue tack.

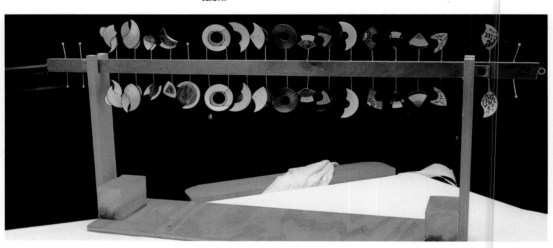

This "blue tack" or "sticky tack" is commercially available (I found it at the local office supply store) and provides a reusable material for supporting the earring while spraying.

If you are making a lot of pieces at one time, you may wish to build a spraying jig like this. The cross member rests in the uprights and can be taken out and set aside to dry.

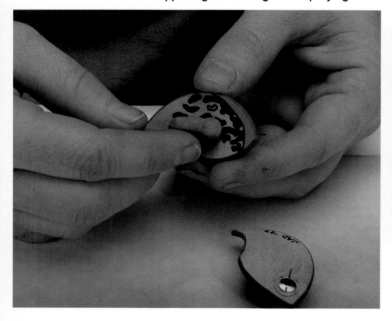

It is gentle enough to use on the decorated surfaces.

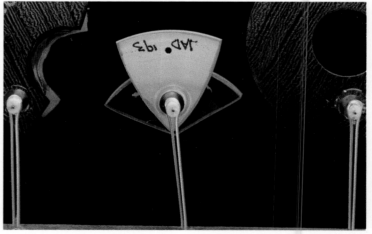

The earring posts are held in a rubber earring back (available at craft stores or through findings suppliers). This is pinched in a cotter pin, which is inserted in the edge of the cross member. With this jig you can spray many pieces at one time, and need not wait for one side to dry before spraying the other.

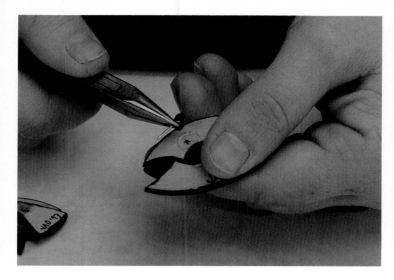

After they are dry, snap the posts off the pieces that are to have pins...

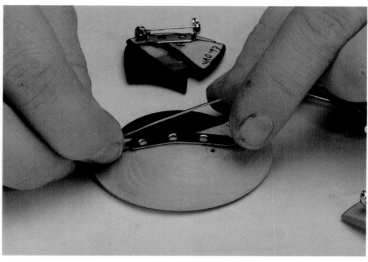

Bend the pin to match the curve of the piece...

and clean away the glue.

and adjust the clutch of the pinback so it will engage the pin.

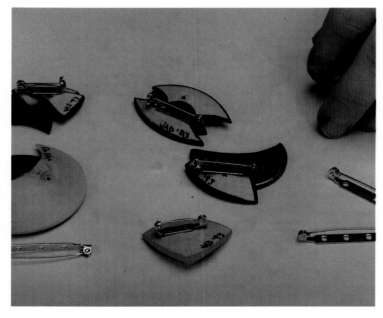

Choose the longest pin back that will fit without showing from the front. This makes the pin hang better on the wearer's clothing.

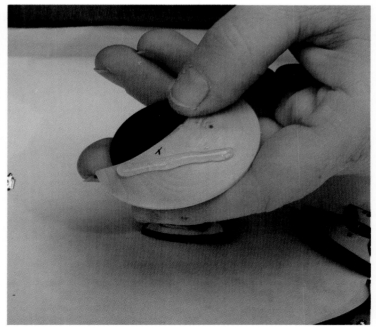

Lay a line of glue where the pin will go...

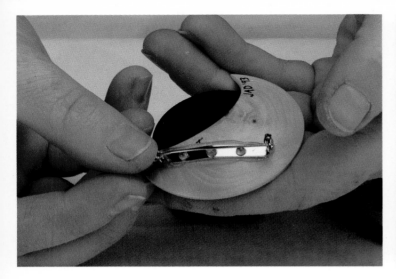

and push the pinback into place. Hold it for a few seconds until the glue sets up.

I usually put a bead between the head of the headpin and the wood. This serves a design function, and the practical purpose of protecting the wood and preventing the wire from being pulled through.

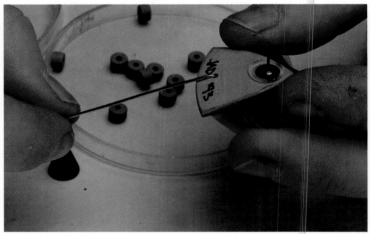

For the beaded pieces the first step is to pick some beads that will complement the design. I keep a large selection of beads on hand. If you are doing only a few pair of earrings it may work better for you to carry your work to a bead shop. Acquiring and maintaining a large variety of beads can become costly!

Bend the wire down at the back of the earring.

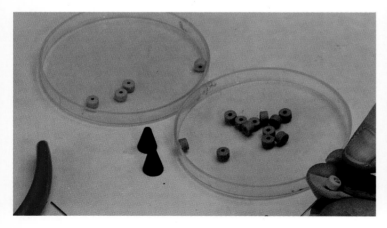

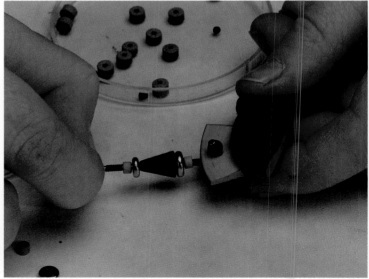

After a principal bead or beads are chosen, I pick out a supporting cast.

The pattern of beads should complement the design of the earring body.

Bend the wire at the desired length.

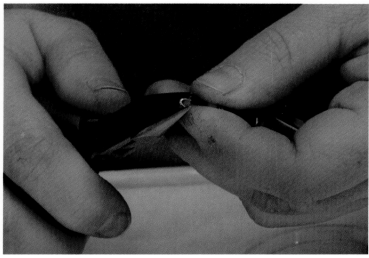

Bend the wire back against itself. This will hold the beads on the wire.

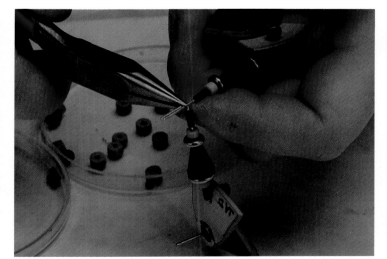

Bend the wire of the other earring in the pair at the same spot.

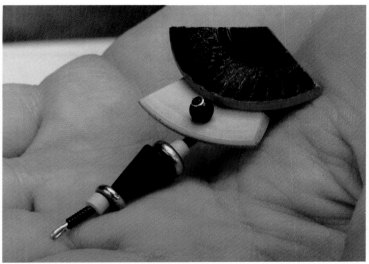

The finished earring.

Finished earrings and pins.

Leaving a little to bend back as a stop, clip off the excess.

Conclusion

In conclusion, I would like to share a few thoughts with you about design, ideas, and copying; and to offer suggestions for ways you might expand your ideas and your work.

The IDEA of making tiny "dishes" on the lathe, cutting and shaping them, and making them into jewelry is not original with me. It was freely given to me and I freely give it to you. I hope you will do as I did -take the idea and use it as a starting place for making your own work.

Mere ideas are a dime a dozen - regular work will generate them abundantly. In addition to fulfilling (in varying degrees!) the design or idea with which you began, each piece you make casts off many alternate, "possible" pieces. Thus, if you are working and paying attention, ideas will proliferate, pardon the expression, like flies in August. Working those ideas out — that is, transforming them into successful pieces — is often long and sometimes difficult work.

If you wish to copy specific designs in this book in order to learn the process, or for your own personal use, that is entirely valid. Copying has a long and legitimate history as a step in learning. But please don't stop there. If you only reproduce my designs and present them as your own - whether to sell at shows, enter competitions, or simply to enjoy the admiration of your handiwork by friends and family - it is not only me you are cheating, but yourself. Indeed, I may never know you have done so, but you will have deprived yourself of pleasure in your own accomplishment, of developing work which has your own heart in it.

The idea of "designing" may seem intimidating - it may call up images of boring hours chained to pencil and paper. Perhaps you think you don't know how to do it or haven't got the "talent". Horsefeathers!

You CAN do it! Think of it not as a tedious chore, but as adventure, exploration, fun. PAY ATTENTION to what you are doing. Try as many things as you can think of, choose the resulting pieces that especially interest you or catch your eye, and pursue the ideas they express.

One advantage of small projects like these is that you can easily afford to try outrageous things. So what if you break a piece or it doesn't go together as you had planned...there you have the beginning of a new plan! If you make a "mistake", LOOK at the result, THINK about what new ideas it may suggest. Look at such occurrences as opportunities to learn something you had not yet thought to look for; or as essayist Wendell Berry writes, as "...occasions for surpassing what [you] know or have reason to expect." You can design with bits of wood as easily as with pencil and paper. Play around with the pieces, especially the ones you think "didn't turn out right." Turn them around, upside down, inside out; draw or write on them, put them together in different ways. When you find something that works, remember it; thus you will add to your "vocabulary", and begin to accumulate a rich storehouse of possible treatments upon which to draw as you work. Soon you'll have many more ideas than time to work them all out.

Just as any map or guide book is only an indication of the realities it represents, this book can only hint at the many directions you may wish to go. Use it not as a simple project plan, but as a tour book, an introduction to possibilities which you will put together according to your own needs, interests, ideas and vision. From the suggestions herein, design your own journey, one that will continue to interest and challenge you. And Bon Voyage!

Gallery

Graphic earrings. Dogwood; pigmented inks. 2.25" x 1.5".

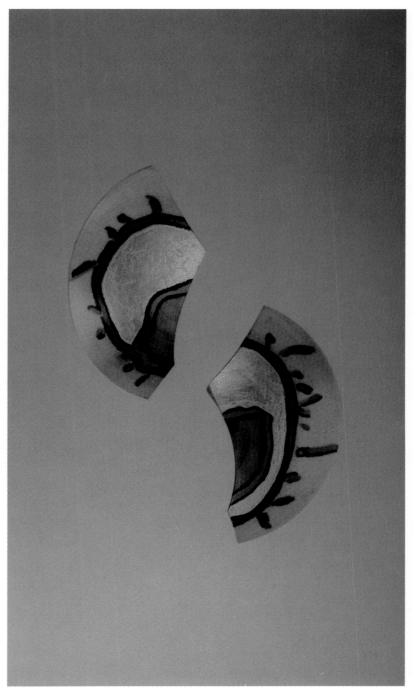

Graphic earrings. Dogwood; pigmented inks. 2" x 1.125".

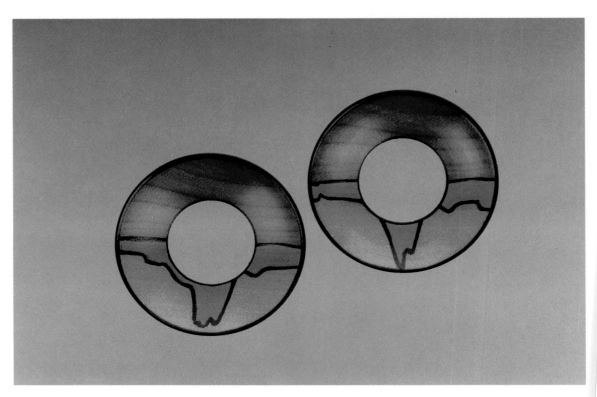

Graphic earrings. Walnut; pigmented inks. 1.75" dia.

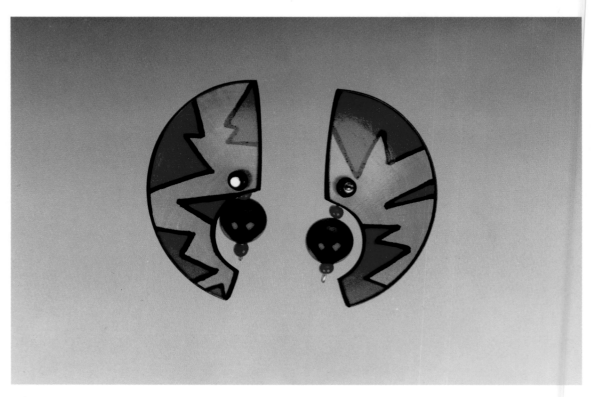

Graphic earrings. American Hornbeam; pigmented inks;
glass, black onyx. 1.5" x .625".

Graphic earrings. Smoketree; pigmented inks. 1.5" dia.

Graphic earrings. Bradford Pear; pigmented inks. .875" x 1.25".

Graphic earrings. Lilac; pigmented inks; porcelain, glass. 1" x .75".

Graphic earrings. Beech; pigmented inks. 2" x 1".

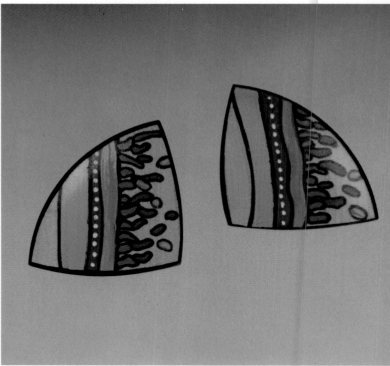

Graphic earrings. Eastern Hophornbeam; pigmented inks. 1" x 1".

Pin. Bocote. 1.5" x 2".

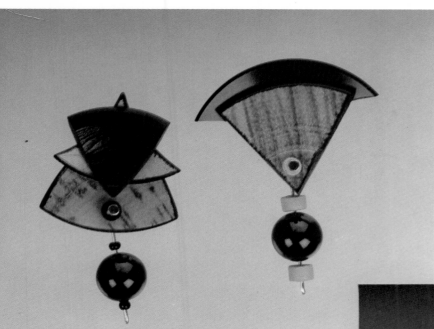

Pins. L: Myrtle, Swamp Privet, ebony; glass, black onyx. 1.25" x 3/4". R: Ebony, Beli; porcelain, black onyx. 1.25" x .75".

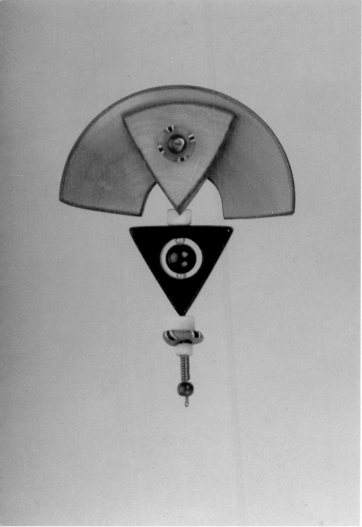

Pin. Spalted Hackberry, Wenge, Desert Ironwood. 2" x 2.125".

Bradford Pear, American Hornbeam; red horn, aja discs, porcelain, glass, niobium, onyx. 1.25" x 1.625".

Pins. L: Myrtle, Ebony w/ chatterwork. 1.75" dia. R: Masur Birch, Greenheart. 1.875" dia.

Pin. Hophornbeam, Ebony w/ chatterwork. 1.875" dia.

Earrings. Ebony, Greenheart. 1.5" x 1.5".

Earrings. Olive; niobium, picture jasper, glass. 2.25" x 1.5".

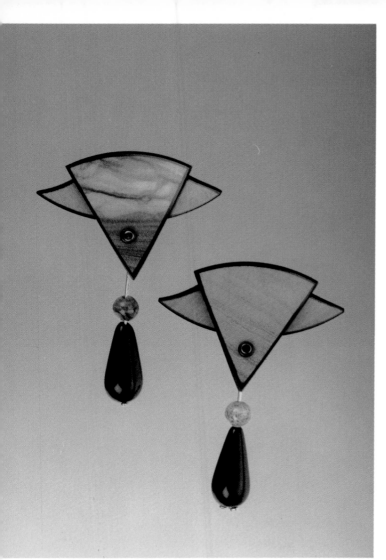

Earrings. Dogwood, Olive. 1.75" x 1".

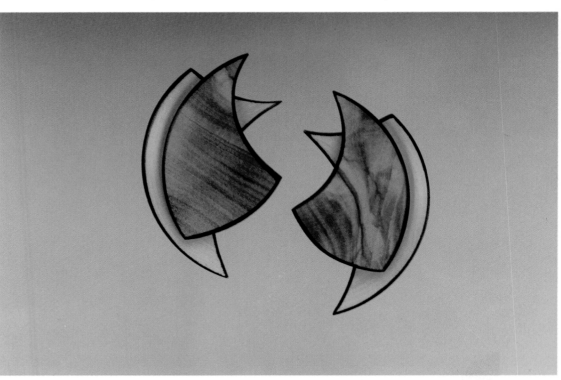

Earrings. Macassar Ebony, Spalted Dogwood; niobium,
hand-blown glass. 2.25" x 1.125".

Earrings. Dogwood. 1.5" x 1.125".

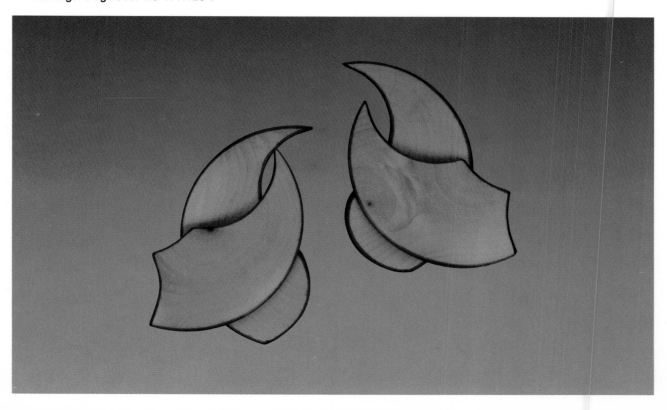

Earrings. Ebony, Spalted Maple; glass, African turquoise. 1.375" x 1".

Earrings. Ebony, Greenheart; niobium, yellow jade, handblown glass. 1.5" x .875".

Earrings. Ebony; Cape amethyst, niobium, black onyx, handblown glass. 1.75" x .875".

Earrings. Swamp Privet, Wenge; porcelain, glass, niobium, handblown glass. 1.375" x .875".

Earrings. Greenheart; aja discs, coco wood, niobium, glass. 1.25" x .75".

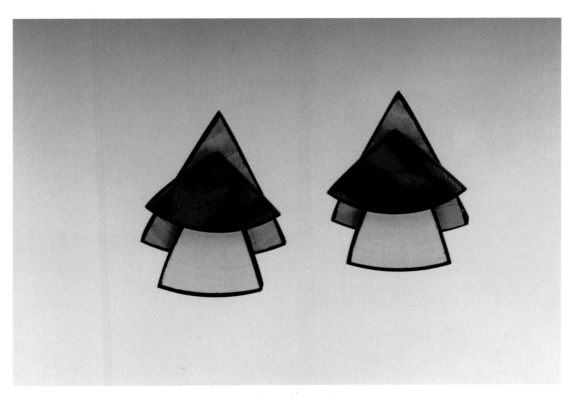

Earrings. Hawthorn, Dogwood, Macassar Ebony. 1.375" x 1.125".

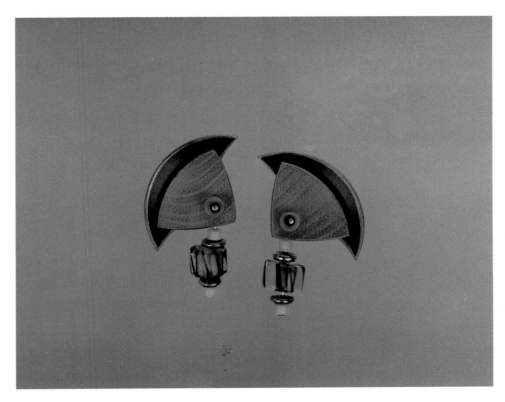

Earrings. Moradillo, Swamp Privet; glass, porcelain, brass, handblown glass. 1.75" x 1".

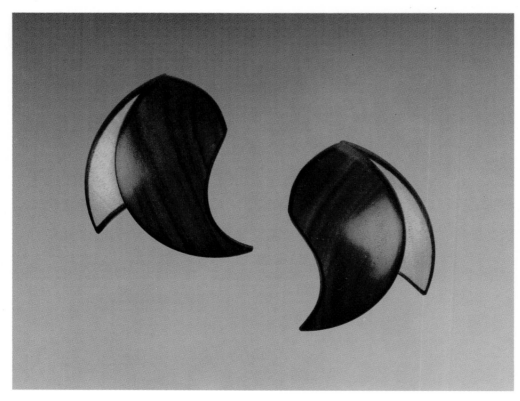

Earrings. Persimmon, Moradillo. 1.5" x 1.25".

Earrings. Bradford Pear, Macassar Ebony w/ chatterwork;
brass, glass, blue lace agate. 1.5" x .75".

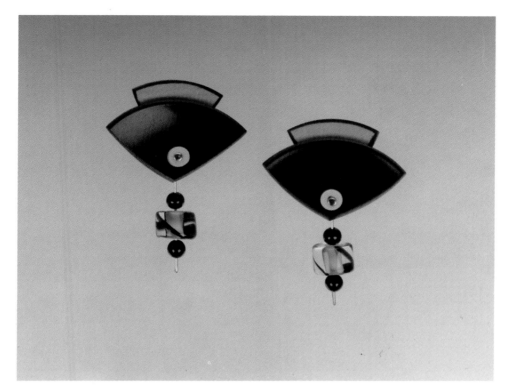

Earrings. Bradford Pear, Ebony; porcelain, black onyx,
handblown glass. 1.625" x 1.25".

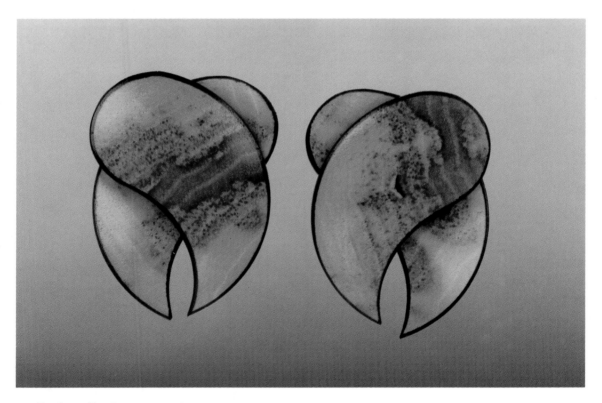

Earrings. Persimmon. 1.75" x 1.25".

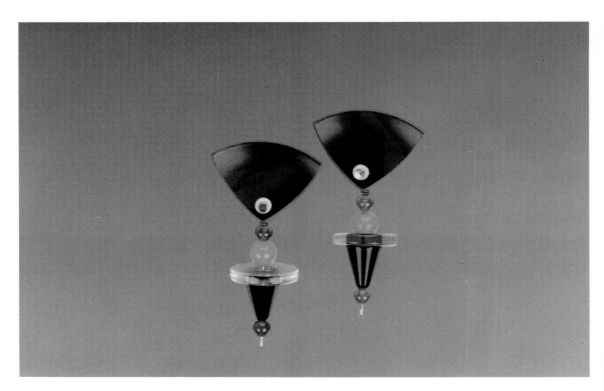

Earrings. Macassar Ebony; porcelain, niobium, Cape
amethyst, yellow jade, handblown glass, blackstone. 2" x 1".

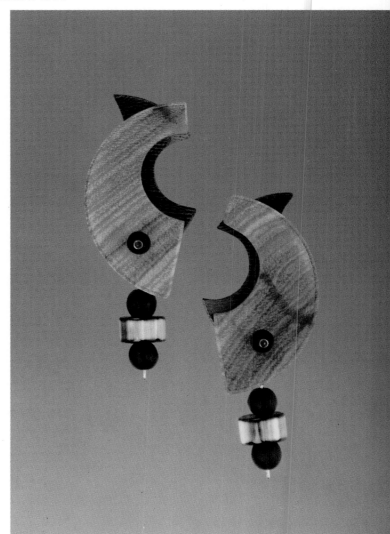

Earrings. Wenge, Beli; glass, handblown glass. 2" x .875".

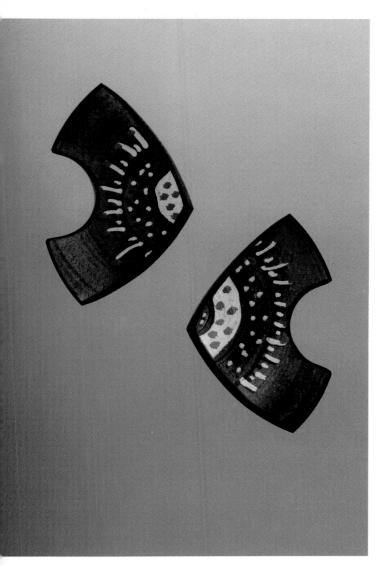

Graphic Earrings. Bradford Pear; pigmented inks. 1.5" x 1".

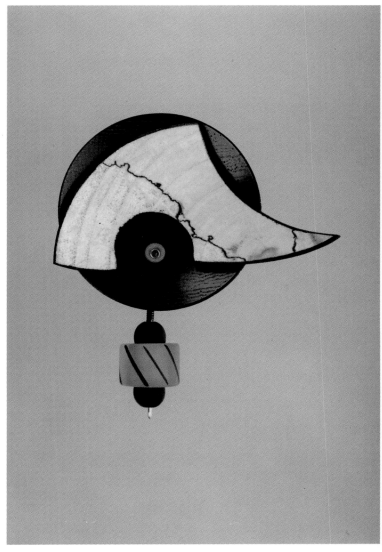

Pin. Wenge, Spalted Hackberry; porcelain, niobium, glass, handblown glass. 2.25" x 2.25".

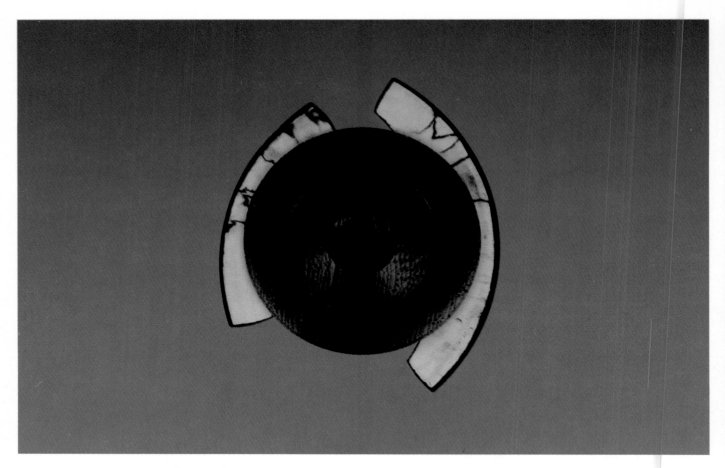

Pin. Spalted Hackberry, Wenge. 2" x 1.75".

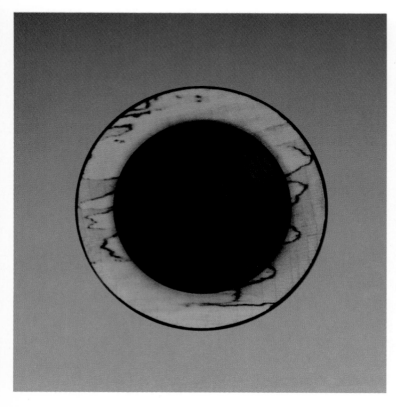

Pin. Spalted Maple, Ebony. 1.875" dia.

Pin. Dogwood, Macassar Ebony. 2" x 1.75".

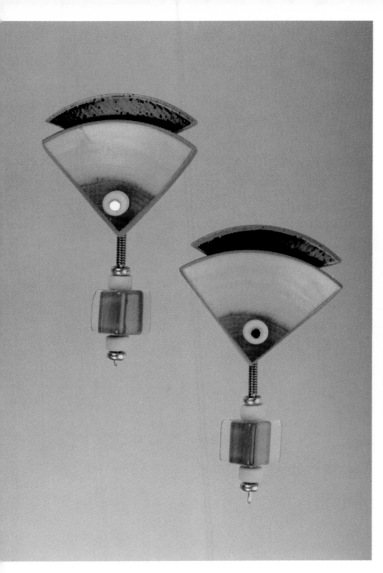

Earrings. Wenge, Apple; niobium, porcelain, brass, handblown glass. 2" x 1.125".

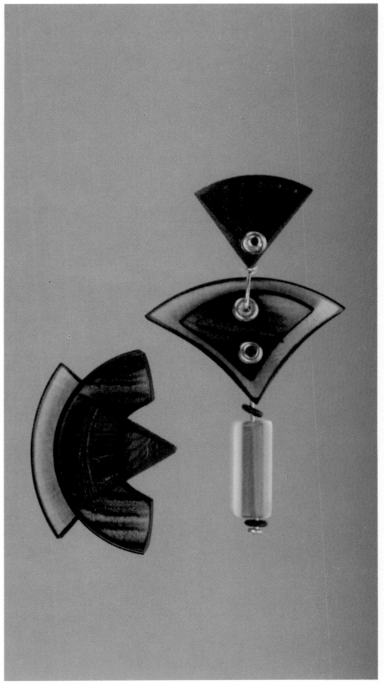

Earrings. Beech, Rosewood, Ebony w/chatterwork; brass, niobium, handblown glass. 1.25" x .75".

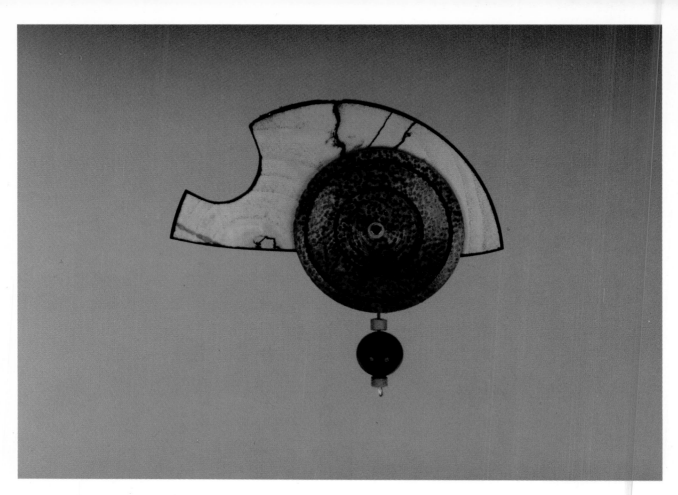

Pin. Spalted Hackberry, Palm; porcelain, black onyx. 2" x
2.25".

Earrings. Wenge, Dogwood; brass, niobium, porcelain,
handblown glass. 2.25" x 1/125".

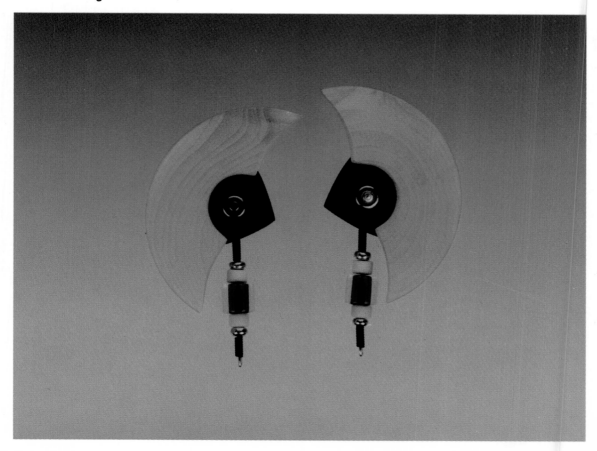

Earrings. Wenge. 1.75" dia.

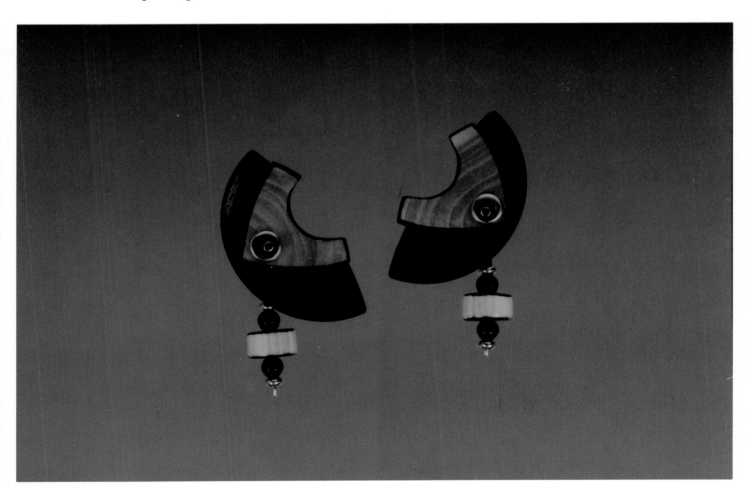

Earrings. Wenge, Hawthorn; glass, brass, black onyx, niobium, handblown glass. 2" x 1".

Earrings. Macassar Ebony, Bradford Pear; brass, coco wood, niobium, porcelain. 2.25" x 1.25".

Earrings. Macassar Ebony, Bradford Pear; pigmented ink. 2" x .75".